PRAYERS

promises

BARBOUR
PUBLISHING

© 2004 by Barbour Publishing, Inc.

ISBN 1-59310-235-6

Cover image © PhotoDisc

Selections are taken from *Prayers & Promises* by Toni Sortor and Pamela McQuade, © 2001 by Barbour Publishing, Inc.; *Prayers & Promises for Men* by John Hudson Tiner, © 2003 by Barbour Publishing, Inc.; *Prayers & Promises for Women* by Toni Sortor, © 2003 by Barbour Publishing, Inc.; and *Prayers & Promises for the Graduate* by Pamela McQuade, © 2003 by Barbour Publishing, Inc.

Unless otherwise noted, Scripture quotations are taken from the King James Version of the Bible.

Scripture quotations marked NIV are taken from the HOLY BIBLE, NEW INTERNATIONAL VERSION®. NIV®. Copyright © 1973, 1978, 1984 by International Bible Society. Used by permission of Zondervan Publishing House. All rights reserved.

Scripture quotations marked NLT are taken from the *Holy Bible*, New Living Translation, copyright © 1996. Used by permission of Tyndale House Publishers, Inc. Wheaton, Illinois 60189, U.S.A. All rights reserved.

Scripture quotations marked NKJV are taken from the New King James Version. Copyright © 1979, 1980, 1982 by Thomas Nelson, Inc. Used by permission. All rights reserved.

Published by Barbour Publishing, Inc., P.O. Box 719, Uhrichsville, Ohio 44683, www.barbourbooks.com

Our mission is to publish and distribute inspirational products offering exceptional value and biblical encouragement to the masses.

ecpa Member of the
Evangelical Christian
Publishers Association

Printed in the United States of America.
5 4 3 2 1

PREFACE

God's promises have richly blessed Christians through the ages. They have offered solutions to problems, strength during trials, and inspiration for the Christian life.

In these pages, we provide ninety-one prayers based on many of Scripture's promises. Whether you are struggling with guilt or fear or need to draw close to God's loving heart, grab hold of a truth in Scripture and share a heartfelt prayer.

Pray, and experience the truth of God's promise to Jeremiah: "Call unto me, and I will answer thee, and show thee great and mighty things, which thou knowest not" (Jeremiah 33:3).

ATTITUDE

Create in me a clean heart, O God;
and renew a right spirit within me.

PSALM 51:10

Father, I am quick to focus on those things that affect me most directly. Often, I confess, I improperly view my wants as essentials. From minor matters such as restaurant service to more important ones such as making major purchases, I insist that my so-called requirements be fully met. I think and act as if those serving me should put my needs first.

Lord, keep a check on my attitude. I want to have a friendly disposition when I deal with others. Create in me a calm, controlled temperament. Help me have a "can do," "everything's okay" attitude rather than a "me" attitude.

AVOIDING DOUBT

Jesus replied, "I tell you the truth,
if you have faith and do not doubt,
not only can you do what was done to the fig tree,
but also you can say to this mountain,
'Go, throw yourself into the sea,'
and it will be done."

MATTHEW 21:21 NIV

It's hard for me to imagine this kind of faith, Lord. So often my own seems to get stuck under mountains instead of moving them. But I know that if You promise such things, they can happen.

Remove my doubt, O Lord. As I trust more fully in You, I know my faith will become strong enough to do Your will. That may not include mountain moving, but I know it can change lives, bring hope, and draw others to You.

Actually, you might call that moving a mountain, after all!

THE BEAUTY
OF HOLINESS

Give unto the LORD the glory due unto his name:
bring an offering, and come before him:
worship the LORD in the beauty of holiness.

1 CHRONICLES 16:29

Holiness is true beauty, not what I wear or how my hair is done or how white my teeth shine. Indeed, holiness is Yours, never mine. I am fatally flawed, but I worship One who is perfect in all ways, One whose glory alone is worthy of praise and thanksgiving. There is no beauty compared to Yours, no faithfulness like Yours. The little glimpses of beauty that decorate my life are grains of silver sand at the edge of an incomprehensible ocean of beauty. I only see a grain or two in my lifetime, but it dazzles my eyes and makes me turn away blinking. I worship You in the beauty of Your holiness.

BELIEVING
WITHOUT SEEING

Whom having not seen, ye love;
in whom, though now ye see him not,
yet believing, ye rejoice with
joy unspeakable and full of glory:
Receiving the end of your faith,
even the salvation of your souls.

1 PETER 1:8–9

I am one of Your peculiar people, Lord, set apart from the world by both my beliefs and my actions. I have never seen even Your sandal prints at the edge of the lake, yet I follow You with all my heart. My ears have never heard Your voice, but I live by Your words. My fingertips have never brushed the edge of Your garment, yet I am healed. My belief is not based in my senses or my intellect but in Your never failing love, which saved my soul and promises me unspeakable joy.

A BROKEN SPIRIT

A merry heart doeth good like a medicine:
but a broken spirit drieth the bones.

PROVERBS 17:22

If a broken spirit dries the bones, Lord, about now mine should be dust. I'm not at all content with my situation, and my heart is down in the dumps. Turn my spirit toward You again, where I can find the joy and contentment I'm missing. May I feel Your Spirit touch my heart so that I may bring good to those I see each day. Help me rejoice in You, no matter what is going on in my life. I don't want sin to turn me into a pile of dry bones, and I don't want to share that attitude with others. Pour Your blessed balm on my aching heart, O Lord.

THE COMPANY OF SINNERS

For I am not come to call the righteous,
but sinners to repentance.

MATTHEW 9:13

Father, examine the way I use my time in Your service. Am I too comfortable? Do I spend my time in fellowship with other believers because it is pleasant and safe, or do I risk the company of sinners? Who needs me most, my neighbor in the pew or my brother and sister in need of repentance and forgiveness? How can I be more effective in my outreach and missionary work?

Your Son showed me by example how I should be spending my time. Give me the strength and courage to make the hard choices, to go where I am needed, to minister to those seemingly beyond help—to risk the company of sinners.

CORRECTION

Stern discipline awaits him who leaves the path;
he who hates correction will die.

PROVERBS 15:10 NIV

Lord, I don't enjoy being corrected, whether it comes from You or from another Christian. I'd rather believe I always do the right thing—but that isn't so. The truth is that to stay on Your narrow path, I need direction from You and wise believers.

Though I don't want to hear correcting words or experience those hard-hitting moments when I know I'm wrong, I know I need them. They seem unpleasant now, but they keep me from falling into greater error and missing Your way entirely.

Help my spirit be gentle enough to accept correction, even when it hurts. I know You only mean it for my benefit. And if I have to correct another Christian, let it be with a kind and righteous spirit.

COUNTING BLESSINGS

Enter into his gates with thanksgiving,
and into his courts with praise:
be thankful unto him, and bless his name.

PSALM 100:4

Dear Lord, what bountiful harvest I have received from You! I count blessings without number. You have given me health, a warm family life, prosperity, and a peaceful heart. You have given me strength in adversity and security in turmoil. You have given me opportunities to serve and thereby enriched my life.

I acknowledge the rich blessings that You have showered upon me. Help me appreciate them. Remove from my heart the idea that my recognition of these blessings will earn me future blessings. Let me focus on what You have done for me and rejoice in all the daily blessings You give me.

DEALING WITH GUILT

I, even I, am he that blotteth out
thy transgressions for mine own sake,
and will not remember thy sins.

Isaiah 43:25

Sometimes, Father, I find myself striving for perfection, certain that I can live a holier life if I only work on myself a little more. Of course what happens is that I make progress on one particular sin at the expense of working on another and end up tormented by guilt.

Remind me that this is not a victory I can ever claim for myself. Sin is with me and will always be with me. Yet You promise that You will not even remember my sins, because You choose not to! You sent Your Son to deal with my sin, and the job has been done. This is not a do-it-yourself project. Thank You, Father.

DEALING WONDROUSLY

And ye shall eat in plenty, and be satisfied,
and praise the name of the LORD your God,
that hath dealt wondrously with you.

JOEL 2:26

You promised to do great things for Israel, Father, even more than You did for them in the past, when You brought them out of Egypt. You would defend them from attack and restore the fruitfulness of the soil, enriching them and guaranteeing them good lives. "The floors shall be full of wheat, and the vats shall overflow with wine and oil" (Joel 2:24). Frightening events would soon take place, but whoever called on the name of the Lord would be delivered. "The LORD will be the hope of his people, and the strength of the children of Israel" (3:16).

Through turmoil and fear, You always protect and save those who love You. You will provide; You will save.

DEFEATING THE ENEMY

"Behold, I give you the authority to
trample on serpents and scorpions,
and over all the power of the enemy,
and nothing shall by any means hurt you."

LUKE 10:19 NKJV

Often, I don't feel much like an overcomer, Lord. Temptation feels very real, and too often I fall into sin. But You look at my spiritual history differently. You see the long haul, both the future and the past; You see the end of my life, as well as the beginning.

You're promising me victory in the end. As I walk faithfully with You, You give me an increasing ability to say "no" to sin. The serpents of temptation fall beneath my feet and no longer harm me.

Nothing hurts me forever when I walk with You, Lord. Keep me strong in clinging to You alone.

THE END

For God so loved the world,
that he gave his only begotten Son,
that whosoever believeth
in him should not perish,
but have everlasting life.

JOHN 3:16

Father, I avoid reading movie or book reviews that go into too much detail about the plot. I enjoy the suspense of waiting to learn how the story unfolds. The ending may be happy or it may have a twist, but I want to be surprised by it.

However, in my own life, I want to know the final result. Thank You, Lord, for telling me the outcome. You have promised that if I seek You, I will find You. Jesus has already paid the penalty for my sins. A faithful life assures me that I will have an eternal home with You.

ENDURANCE

But he that shall endure unto the end,
the same shall be saved.

MATTHEW 24:13

Lord, I must admit that words like *patience* and *endurance* aren't my favorites. They make me think of gritting my teeth and bearing up under troubles—and I never look forward to troubles.

Give me Your vision of patience and endurance, Jesus. You came to earth and bore my sins, when heaven was Your rightful home. You endured much on earth so that I could relate to You. Help me see the value in patiently enduring hardship. I look forward with joy to eternity with You. Strengthen me, Lord, to be patient until that day.

EVERLASTING TRUTH

*"The grass withers, and the flowers fade,
but the word of our God stands forever."*

ISAIAH 40:8 NLT

So much changes in life, Lord. Just when I think I'm secure, I can almost count on some fluctuation, and my world becomes different again. Just as the seasons alter and the flowers die off, life is constantly moving.

But Your truths aren't one thing in the summer season and another in fall. Your Word doesn't say one thing this month and something new ninety days later. It always shows me what You are like and never changes. I can count on Scripture always to be truthful and to lead me in the right path.

Thank You, Lord, for sharing Your everlasting truth with me. Help me to be steadfast in clinging to Your way.

EVIDENCE

Now faith is the substance of things hoped for,
the evidence of things not seen.

HEBREWS 11:1

Lord, astronomers have recently discovered distant moons and planets they cannot see through even the strongest of telescopes. By observing the effects these bodies have on other bodies—changes in orbit, for example—they know these distant bodies simply must be there, or their effects would not be there. This is "evidence of things not seen," perhaps even the "substance of things hoped for." I admit I do not totally understand how the astronomers do this, but I find it comforting.

There is so much I do not understand about You. Still, I can see the effects of Your actions, the evidence that You are still active in my daily life and the lives of others. I do not need to physically see You to believe. Your evidence is everywhere.

FEELING FAR FROM GOD

*But if from there you seek the LORD your God,
you will find him if you look for him
with all your heart and with all your soul.*

DEUTERONOMY 4:29 NIV

Sometimes when I hurt, I feel so far from You, Lord, that I begin to wonder if You even care anymore. When I experience that feeling, often it's because the world has gotten in between us. I've fallen into sin, and the sin looks good. Or I've let the sand of being overly busy keep me from time with You. Forgive me, Lord.

A life off course becomes a lonely existence. Even in a crowd, I feel far from everyone. All I need to do is return to You. Turn my heart again in the right direction, Lord. Help me put aside all that divides us and draw close to Your side again.

FINDING LIFE

"Whoever finds his life will lose it,
and whoever loses his life
for my sake will find it."

MATTHEW 10:39 NIV

The new life You promise, Lord, isn't simply for a few years—not even one hundred of them. Your life lasts forever, and I will share eternity with You. That's why You tell me not to cling too closely to this world. Eternity doesn't depend on my going with the crowd here on earth, because their choices don't last. It doesn't require that I please anyone but You.

I want to use this life to make a difference for eternity. In the here and now I can share Your love with those who don't yet know You and those who struggle to live their new lives well. Whatever I lose in this world, let it be for gain in Your kingdom.

FINDING
THE SHORELINE

Thy word is a lamp unto my feet,
and a light unto my path.

PSALM 119:105

If there's one thing I need, it's trustworthy guidance, Lord. There is plenty of advice available to me in these modern times. The Internet is full of it—some good, some bad. If I prefer hard copy, thousands of books are published every year on religion and ethics. Even television offers all types of advice for all types of problems, if I take it to heart or not. If I took all the advice I hear seriously, I would be driven like a wave from one place to another without ever finding the shoreline. There is only one way to reach the path to the beach: trusting in Your Word. In darkness or light, on fair days or foul, I can trust the light of Your Word to bring me safely home.

FORGIVING LOVE

"Don't tear your clothing in your grief;
instead, tear your hearts."
Return to the LORD your God,
for he is gracious and merciful.
He is not easily angered.
He is filled with kindness and
is eager not to punish you.

JOEL 2:13 NLT

When I've done wrong, it's comforting to know You want me to return to You, Lord. Though it seems right that You should hold my sin against me, that's not Your desire. You've already forgiven my sin with Jesus' sacrifice. I need simply turn to You and acknowledge my unfaithfulness.

Turn my heart from wrongdoing, Lord. I don't want to miss out on a moment of Your love and grace. Draw me close, Jesus, to Your wounded side, where I can rejoice in Your forgiving love.

THE GENUINE ARTICLE

Whatsoever things are true,
whatsoever things are honest,
whatsoever things are just,
whatsoever things are pure,
whatsoever things are lovely,
whatsoever things are of good report
. . .think on these things.

PHILIPPIANS 4:8

Father, I can see in my daily activities how people strive for easy perfection—a mathematical "proof" that solves a problem in the least number of steps, a musical composition without a discordant note, a work of art that achieves harmony and symmetric composition.

Dear Lord, I strive for a life in tune with Your orchestration. I know that to have an honorable life, I must be meticulous in eliminating the inferior elements and strive to reflect Your higher nature. I want to be a genuine Christian. I put my life in Your hands so that I can come closer to reaching that goal.

GIVING IN FAITH

But when thou makest a feast,
call the poor, the maimed, the lame, the blind:
And thou shalt be blessed;
for they cannot recompense thee:
for thou shalt be recompensed at
the resurrection of the just.

LUKE 14:13–14

Father, sometimes charity seems to be a thankless task. No one will ever repay me, and I see no immediate results to give me some sense of satisfaction. It's like dropping a penny into a bottomless well: I can't even hear it *clink* at the end of its fall.

Remind me that though the little I can give seems useless, when added to the little that millions give, my charity can make a difference. You recall every penny I drop into the alms box; the consequences of my charity are in Your hands. Help me to give in faith.

GIVING OF MYSELF

And whosoever will be chief among you,
let him be your servant:
Even as the Son of man came
not to be ministered unto, but to minister,
and to give his life a ransom for many.

MATTHEW 20:27–28

As I contemplate all the activities that demand my attention, I think of You, Jesus. You did the work of a servant by washing the feet of the apostles. Please help me remember that the greatest in the kingdom of heaven is not the one being served, but the humble one doing the serving.

Sometimes I find it easier to give from a distance than to become personally involved in situations. Help me, Lord, to fulfill the mission to serve others. I need Your strength to meet my obligations to my family, my coworkers, and members of my community.

GOD OWNS
ALL CREATION

The earth is the LORD's,
and everything in it.
The world and all its people belong to him.

PSALM 24:1 NLT

Thank You, Lord, for controlling all creation, though things can seem so confused. I often wonder where this world is going, but I'm glad I can trust in Your control over all living things.

Even people, whom You created along with the birds, bees, and other creatures, are under Your control. Though they may not all glorify You with their lives, they cannot do anything to set aside Your command of creation. Their wickedness cannot destroy Your plans for Your world.

Thank You for owning me, along with everything else. I'm incredibly glad to belong to the Lord of the universe.

GOD'S CHILDREN

*For his Holy Spirit speaks to us deep in our hearts
and tells us that we are God's children.*

ROMANS 8:16 NLT

No matter what happens to my family, Lord, Your Spirit has promised that I'm never alone. I'm always part of Your family, which may have members who get closer to my heart than some of my blood relatives. If I lost everyone You've given me—my parents, brothers, sisters, and my extended family—I'd never be alone. Thank You for caring so much for my heart that You bring me family members who love You, whether or not they're related by blood.

I'm glad to be part of Your family. Help me become a child You can be proud of, Lord.

GOD'S DIRECTION

Trust in the LORD with all thine heart;
and lean not unto thine own understanding.
In all thy ways acknowledge him,
and he shall direct thy paths.

PROVERBS 3:5–6

I never know what the day will bring, Lord. A perfectly ordinary day may end with glory or grief, or it may end like a perfectly ordinary day usually ends. I try to prepare myself for anything that comes my way, at least mentally; but the truth is, there are too many possibilities for me to even consider. All I can do is put my trust in You and live each day in the belief that You know how everything will work out—even if I don't. You will show me which way to turn. You will guide and protect me day after day. You have a plan; and although I don't know or understand it, I trust in You.

GOD'S HONESTY

"And he who is the Glory of Israel will not lie,
nor will he change his mind,
for he is not human that
he should change his mind!"

1 SAMUEL 15:29 NLT

How glad I am, Lord, that I can trust You not to lie or change Your thinking. You follow through on every promise, and nothing ever alters Your perfection.

You want me to be honest because that's what You are; and as I grow in You, I must increasingly reflect Your nature. Help me to become completely reliable. When I tell a friend I'll help out, I want him to be able to count on me. When a coworker needs the truth, let her be able to turn to me.

Every day, make me more like You, Lord. In my own strength, I'm only human; but Your Spirit makes me ever more like You.

GOD'S JUSTICE

*"Have nothing to do with a false charge
and do not put an innocent or honest person
to death, for I will not acquit the guilty."*

EXODUS 23:7 NIV

When sin harms an innocent person, it's easy to wonder where You are, Lord. "Why did this happen?" I ask. "Why wasn't it stopped?"

Verses like this give me hope, though. You warn Your people not to do evil because You will not acquit them. How much less will You acquit someone who has no regard for You or relationship with You.

When I can't see Your justice, help me still to trust in it. Let me know a response is on its way, even if You don't show it before I meet with eternity.

GOD'S PROMISES
ARE SURE

He hath given meat unto them that fear him:
he will ever be mindful of his covenant.

PSALM 111:5

Father, being human, with human weaknesses, we may forget our promises to our children, but You never forget Your promises to us. You remain honorable and full of compassion even when we are weak and easily frightened. Your commandments stand forever, as does the redemption of Your people through Jesus Christ. Out of Your great mercy, You will always provide for those who love You and follow Your ways. Remind me of this when I am in need of food or shelter, Lord. Sometimes my needs seem to be the most important things in my life, but I know this is only panic speaking. I need never panic again: Your promises are sure. Help my desperation of today give way to Your reassurance and love.

THE GOLDEN RULE

Therefore all things whatsoever
ye would that men should do to you,
do ye even so to them:
for this is the law and the prophets.

MATTHEW 7:12

Lord, I have memorized the Bible verse that is called the Golden Rule. Yet, putting it into practice is far more difficult than learning the words. While You were here on earth, You demonstrated the perfect example of living out this principle.

Jesus, I praise You for showing me compassion and granting me forgiveness for my transgressions. Thank You for teaching me how to have peace in my life. Lord, give me the determination to do unto others as I want them to do unto me.

FOR GOVERNMENT LEADERS

I exhort therefore, that, first of all,
supplications, prayers, intercessions,
and giving of thanks, be made for all men;
For kings, and for all that are in authority;
that we may lead a quiet and peaceable life
in all godliness and honesty.

1 TIMOTHY 2:1–2

Heavenly Father, I ask that You guide the leaders of my country. May they have integrity, morality, and leadership ability. Guide them to extend Your influence into all areas of society. Empower them to overcome the dark forces at work in the world.

Father, I ask for Your guidance upon my government's leaders. Direct them to take our nation in the way You would have us go. Help them realize that true prosperity comes only through the application of Christian values. May the laws they make uphold and protect our right to worship You.

GREATNESS IN SERVICE

"The greatest among you
will be your servant."

MATTHEW 23:11 NIV

It's hard to think of greatness in servanthood, Lord. Our world doesn't think that way, and breaking out of the mold takes effort. Even in church I can have a hard time seeing greatness as a matter of doing things for others.

Help me change my thinking, Jesus, and help me model the lifestyle You want every Christian to have. Instead of seeking personal fame or self-importance, I need to help others and aid them in drawing closer to You. When other people see my actions, I want them to see You.

Help me become Your servant in every way, Lord. Then I'll have the only greatness worth having—I will be distinguished in Your eyes.

HEALED BY JESUS

But he was wounded for our transgressions,
he was bruised for our iniquities:
the chastisement of our peace was upon him;
and with his stripes we are healed.

<small>ISAIAH 53:5</small>

Lord, I do not even know how many times You have already restored my health. I may have never seen or understood many of Your actions, and I may often credit others for what was actually Your healing and preservation. But I know You are always with me, and I thank You for Your protection.

Father God, whether it's a physical sickness or a spiritual one, You have promised I have healing in Jesus. No illness is beyond Your power, Lord. When I suffer from sin or physical pain, keep me mindful that Your hand is still on me. May each trial strengthen me spiritually and draw me nearer to You. Ultimately, I will experience Your healing—here or in heaven.

Keep me mindful of the price Your Son paid so I could enjoy a healthy relationship with You. Let my trust in You never fail.

HEART PURITY

Blessed are the pure in heart:
for they shall see God.

MATTHEW 5:8

When purity of heart, mind, and soul seems difficult, remind me of this promise, Lord. Seeing You is the greatest blessing I could receive— I especially long to look directly into Your face.

In this world, I cannot see You fully, though every day I perceive more of Your love, grace, and blessing as I draw nearer to You in obedience. I cannot see You physically, yet I get a clearer spiritual picture of You every day as I live out Your commands. Reading Your Word, praying, and acting in a way that pleases You make You ever clearer to my heart and soul.

Make my heart increasingly pure, Lord. Long before we meet face-to-face I want to know You well.

HIDDEN STRENGTH

He gives strength to the weary
and increases the power of the weak.

ISAIAH 40:29 NIV

I am not courageous, Lord. Like a child, sometimes I still wonder about the monsters under the bed and turn on every light in the house as soon as the sun sets. When I look at my life's challenges, I feel so small and inadequate.

Yet You promise courage and strength when I need them. Sometimes, in Your power, I even do remarkable things that cannot be explained; I can rise to great heights when necessary. After the danger is passed, my knees may give out, and I wonder how I did such wonders. Then the light dawns: You did wonders through me. Thank You for the hidden strength You give me—Your strength.

HOPE IN TROUBLE

But the needy will not always be forgotten,
nor the hope of the afflicted ever perish.

PSALM 9:18 NIV

I certainly have needs now, Lord. They overwhelm me until I hardly know where to turn.

But I still hope in You, Jesus. I know You will never forget me or desert me, and You will always provide a way out of my troubles. No matter what problems we have faced, You have never yet forgotten or given up on Your people. Though it may take some time, You faithfully respond.

In my need, assuage my physical and spiritual emptiness, Lord. To have one need fulfilled without the other will not make me complete. Without Your Spirit's flow in my life, I am still afflicted. I need Your filling, Lord.

AN INSTANT WORLD

For ye have need of patience, that,
after ye have done the will of God,
ye might receive the promise.

HEBREWS 10:36

This is an instant world, Lord. Patience is not much valued here. If I don't get what I think I need, I take charge myself and double my efforts, not even thinking about sitting back in patience and waiting for You to act. Like a little child, I run to and fro looking for something to amuse me, even when I know it's not amusement I need. Just like a child, I get myself in trouble when I run ahead of You. On days when I go off on my own, draw me close to You until I calm down and begin to think clearly. Everything is under control. All I need has been provided. All I need to contribute is faith and patience.

JESUS' FRIENDS

"You are my friends if you do what I command."

JOHN 15:14 NIV

Friendship with You, Lord, should mean the most to me. When I run out the door to be with another friend, I shouldn't leave You behind. Wherever we go, You can be a welcome third, who enjoys and blesses our fellowship.

Whatever I do, help me remember that Your friendship means more than any human relationship. I can't share with others the way I can with You; I'd never tell anyone else all the secrets of my heart. No one knows me as You do, even when I don't understand myself.

What You command, Lord, I want to do, whether I'm with others or alone. Help me and my friends to obey You always.

THE "KISS" PRINCIPLE

But I fear, lest by any means,
as the serpent beguiled Eve
through his subtilty,
so your minds should be corrupted
from the simplicity that is in Christ.

2 CORINTHIANS 11:3

Lord, the management principle known as KISS—"Keep It Simple, Stupid"—does have its merits, despite the "Stupid" reference. I am involved in far too many organizations and activities that litter my mind and fritter away my time.

Father, I long for simplicity in my relationship with You. Please help me manage my time so I can focus on a better kinship with You. Release me from the clutter of unimportant activities that infringe on my time and attention. I pray that I will set aside quiet time for reflection and communication with You.

LABORERS WITH GOD

For we are labourers together with God:
ye are God's husbandry,
ye are God's building.

1 CORINTHIANS 3:9

The best thing about working is knowing I'm not working alone. I may plant the seeds, but You water them. I may do the weeding, but You send the sunshine. All I am and all I do is done with You, the One who created me and gifted me with whatever skills I have. You give my work—whatever type of work it may be—dignity and purpose. Your faith in me enables me to continue my duties on days when I would otherwise despair. At the end of the day my feet may be burning, but I know I am walking in Your footsteps, and that gives me peace. I thank You for the work I have. May I do it in a way that is pleasing to You and reflects Your glory.

LIGHT'S POWER

The light shines through the darkness,
and the darkness can never extinguish it.

JOHN 1:5 NLT

Your light will never be extinguished, Lord. No evil or power of Satan can overpower Your strength. No depraved man overcomes Your will. Nothing wicked conquers Your love, power, and wisdom.

Remind me of that truth when overcoming sin seems hard. Instead of thinking that I have to overcome, I must remember I have no such ability. Nothing in me pierces the darkness; only Your power pushes back Satan's murkiness and brings me into Your pure light.

Without Your light, I'm lost, Jesus. Fill me with Your brightness, and use my life to do Your work of eradicating the darkness in the world around me.

A LIVING STONE

Ye also, as lively stones,
are built up a spiritual house,
an holy priesthood,
to offer up spiritual sacrifices,
acceptable to God by Jesus Christ.

1 PETER 2:5

Lord, I am amazed at the ceaseless action of waves. I find stones that are rounded smooth by the continuous pounding of the water. Even the edges of broken glass are smoothed away until they are no longer sharp.

Father, I see Your ceaseless action on my life in the same way. Day by day, You remove my rough edges. You blunt my sharp tongue, soften my overbearing manner, cool my hot temper, and smooth out my uneven disposition. From a rough and unremarkable stone, You have made me into something better. Thank You for continuously changing me.

THE LORD DELIVERS

The Lord knoweth how to deliver
the godly out of temptations.

2 PETER 2:9

Self-control is not an easy path to follow. Those of us who try to follow You know it is steep, the footing insecure. Often it seems that others are standing at the edge of the path and throwing rocks under my feet, just to watch me stumble. If I lose my footing and fall, they take great pleasure in mocking me. Without Your help, I would fail to reach my goal; but You have promised that You will be there for me when I call for help. I do not know how to deliver myself from temptation, but You know the way. You have been there. You suffered temptation and won all Your trials. When I stumble, Your arms catch me; if I fall, You bring me to my feet and guide me onward.

LOVE

Know therefore that the LORD thy God,
he is God, the faithful God,
which keepeth covenant and mercy
with them that love him
and keep his commandments
to a thousand generations.

DEUTERONOMY 7:9

Omnipotent Father, there are no limitations to the amount of love and attention You can bestow upon each of Your children. Although I receive Your rich blessings all the time, day and night, I pray that I will not take Your love for granted.

Lord, the more I know You and understand You, the more I will see and appreciate Your love. I pray that I will experience You more deeply so that my love for You will increase. You have taught me that sacrifices must be made for love to grow. I submit to You. Demolish me and then rebuild me so I may be one with You.

LOVE'S COURAGE

O love the LORD, all ye his saints:
for the LORD preserveth the faithful,
and plentifully rewardeth the proud doer.
Be of good courage,
and he shall strengthen your heart,
all ye that hope in the LORD.

PSALM 31:23–24

When my courage seems so small and slips away, when sin seeks to pull me from Your path, Lord, remind me of these verses. I need only trust in You, the One who keeps me safe and brings good things into my life. You reward my feeble efforts and multiply them through Your strength as I simply love You and respond to You in faith.

I want to be strong—in You and for You. Give me courage each day. When evil seems to abound and sin distracts me from Your way, thank You that Your love abounds still more.

MY REACTIONS

If ye endure chastening,
God dealeth with you as with sons;
for what son is he whom
the father chasteneth not?

HEBREWS 12:7

•

You are my perfect Father, but I am Your imperfect child, full of human failings and sometimes in need of correction. If You did not love me, You would ignore my misdeeds, leaving me to my own devices and letting the chips fall where they may, but You do not do this. You love me and therefore correct me, as I do with my own children.

Like my children, I do not always welcome correction. I pout; I avoid You; I try to go my own way. I even say, "It's not my fault!" as if I were not responsible for my own actions. In times like these, be patient with me, Father, because I cannot live without Your love.

NOT FORSAKEN

But I am poor and needy;
yet the Lord thinketh upon me.

PSALM 40:17

Who am I to come to You with prayers and thanksgiving, Lord? Who cares what I think? I am not a great person—not even a particularly good person. I will never do wonderful things or be loved by everyone who knows me. I will spend my life in loneliness and fear, just another nobody in a world full of nobodies.

But still You think about me. You don't just notice me and pass on—You actually take the time to think about me, to pay attention to me, to help me when I need help, and to protect me when I need protecting. I am not alone; I am not forsaken. Thank You, Lord!

NOTHING NEW

I have seen all the works
that are done under the sun;
and, behold, all is vanity
and vexation of spirit.

ECCLESIASTES 1:14

Each day, Lord, I am bombarded with advertisements. Embedded in the glittering generalities is the assurance that the merchandise is on the leading edge. The fashion models are chosen because of their appeal to the young and vigorous. I suddenly discover a product that is essential, although I have been getting along without it all of my life. I disparage as outdated my perfectly serviceable possessions.

Heavenly Father, I pray that I will not allow advertisements to exploit my tendency to be discontented. Help me dismiss sales pitches that appeal to desire and pride. Keep me away from the idea that I can improve my future with things rather than by living for You.

OUR SOURCE OF STRENGTH

The righteous also shall hold on his way,
and he that hath clean hands
shall be stronger and stronger.

JOB 17:9

On my own, I am rarely as strong as I need to be, Lord. Sickness weakens me; cares and worry tire my mind and make me less productive than I want to be. Old age will eventually defeat my body. Even when I am physically fit, I know there is weakness in me. But You promise that I will be able to continue in Your Way as long as I have faith and I trust Your promises. Make me stronger every day, Lord, no matter how heavy my burdens may be. Show me all the good You have done for the faithful throughout history, and give me some of Your strength when my own fails. Let my dependence on You turn weakness into strength.

THE PATHWAY

And thine ears shall hear
a word behind thee, saying,
This is the way, walk ye in it,
when ye turn to the right hand,
and when ye turn to the left.

ISAIAH 30:21

If life is like a pathway in the woods, I'm always making problems for myself along the way. The woods are deep and dark, and I am easily distracted. I go off to the left to find a hidden spring that I can hear bubbling up, only to lose the path. I follow the tracks of a deer until sunset and barely find shelter before darkness falls. I make the same mistakes on the path of life, losing sight of the trail and calling out for You to find me before it's too late and I am lost forever.

Thank You for finding me, Lord, for putting my feet back on the path and leading me home.

PEACE

When a man's ways please the LORD,
he maketh even his enemies
to be at peace with him.

PROVERBS 16:7

Lord, You know I want my ways to please You.
Serving You is the greatest thing I can do with
my life. As an added benefit, You have promised that
because I obey, You will smooth my path. Even my
enemies will become peaceful.

I've already seen Your promise at work in my life.
Sometimes, when life seems to be getting rough, I
pray—and the path becomes smooth before me.
Issues I thought would become real problems turn
into nothing at all, and I know You have answered
my prayer.

Thank You for Your peace, which goes before me
every day to bless my life.

PERSISTENT PRAYER

"Ask, and it will be given to you;
seek, and you will find;
knock, and it will be opened to you.
For everyone who asks receives,
and he who seeks finds,
and to him who knocks it will be opened."

MATTHEW 7:7–8 NKJV

I've asked for things in prayer and not gotten them, Lord. Then I've started to wonder if I should have asked at all. But this verse encourages me not only to ask once, but to seek and knock persistently for the good things of Your kingdom.

When I don't get an immediate answer, Lord, remind me to check with You to make sure my request is good—and then to keep on trusting and persisting. You don't ignore my prayers, even if I don't get the response I'd wanted. You will answer when the time is right.

Thank You, Lord, for Your answers to every prayer.

THE PERSON WITHIN

*For man looketh on the outward appearance,
but the LORD looketh on the heart.*

1 SAMUEL 16:7

We are too conscious of outward beauty today, Lord. Our singers, our heroes, our role models —even our politicians—are expected to meet certain standards of beauty. Even worse, we instinctively trust the beautiful, never looking beyond their bodies, as though perfect hair indicates a perfect brain or a pure heart. When we stop to think about it, we know this is foolish, but we rarely do think about it. Make me more conscious of this error, Lord. Teach me to look through appearance when I choose my heroes or my spouse. A perfect hairdo should not unduly influence me—it may be warming a very small brain. An expensive Italian suit may very well be covering a dark heart. Help me see beyond beauty—or the lack of it.

A PERSONAL PRAYER

And this is life eternal,
that they might know thee the only true God,
and Jesus Christ, whom thou hast sent.

JOHN 17:3

Heavenly Father, in this prayer I want to speak to You about myself. I pray that it is not a selfish prayer, for my ultimate goal is to be right with You. Please make a way for me to avoid sin and help me to accept Your forgiveness when I do sin. I long to be right with You. Direct my steps to always be in the path of righteousness.

Father, help me recognize the work You have given me to do, and assist me as I try to glorify You. Stamp Your name on my heart so that I may live eternally in Your presence.

THE PICTURE JESUS SEES

According as he hath chosen us in him
before the foundation of the world,
that we should be holy and without blame
before him in love.

EPHESIANS 1:4

Dear Lord, with an auto-everything camera, even I can take pictures. But I have found that snapping the shutter does not guarantee a good photo. I've learned to aim the camera to cut out distracting elements such as road signs, to avoid trees growing out of heads, and to keep power lines from cutting across a scenic view. Sometimes I have to use a flash to illuminate a dark subject.

Jesus, in Your honored position of viewing earth from heaven, what kind of image of my life do You see? Remove all distracting elements from my Christian character. Illuminate me with Your love, and frame me in Your Word. I pray You will compose my life so it presents a pleasing picture to others—and to You.

PLANNING

A man's heart deviseth his way:
but the LORD directeth his steps.

PROVERBS 16:9

I have made lots of plans in my lifetime, Father, some of them just wishful thinking, some very concrete and detailed. They were all good mental discipline, but not all that many worked out the way I thought they would. Some I was not at all suited for; others would take me two lifetimes to complete. Still, it's good to have some idea of where I want to go and what I will need along the way. Not all my plans are in Your will, though—even those that sound like good ideas to me. When they are not, You show me a better idea, and I thank You for Your guidance. Keep me on the right path when my own plans are flawed, because only You know where You need me to be today and tomorrow.

POSSIBILITIES

All things are possible to him that believeth.

MARK 9:23

What an amazing promise this is, Lord! I can hardly believe You wrote this to me. You've opened so many doors to me simply because I have faith in You.

I know that amazing promise doesn't mean I can demand anything I want. There are plenty of wrong things in this world—or things that would simply be wrong for me—that Your promise doesn't automatically cover. But You have given me an open door to all the good things You offer me, all the positive things that I can do, and all the challenges You want me to overcome.

When it comes to the things You say are right, I don't want to think too small. All things are possible in You.

THE POWER
OF THE WORD

For our gospel came not unto you in word only,
but also in power, and in the Holy Ghost,
and in much assurance;
as ye know what manner of men we were
among you for your sake.

1 THESSALONIANS 1:5

Lord, I confess to You that I often read the Bible hurriedly and without much comprehension. Despite my sometimes superficial reading, I do gain something from staying in touch with You. More gratifying, though, are those occasions when I take the time to think upon Your Word and meditate upon Your message. Most useful of all are those occasions when certain passages capture my attention. For several days I carry the verses around in my thoughts and pray about them. Slowly, by continually holding them in my mind, they dawn into full light.

Father, I pray that the power of Your Word will transform my mind. Change the printed words into words written on my heart and living in my spirit.

PRAISE IN
THE ASSEMBLY

To appoint unto them that mourn in Zion,
to give unto them beauty for ashes,
the oil of joy for mourning,
the garment of praise for the spirit of heaviness
. . .that he might be glorified.

ISAIAH 61:3

Thank You, Lord, that in Your wisdom You have given me Your day as a reminder to rest and renew. As I assemble with other believers, the stresses of the week dissipate. I feel Your living Spirit as the unified body of Christ worships You.

I thank You, Lord, for allowing me to be a part of the assembly, where the cares of the week are put aside. There is joy in my heart as I leave Your house. Fellowship with other believers ignites a fire that burns in my heart throughout the week.

A PRAYER
FOR THOSE IN NEED

Blessed is he that considereth the poor:
the LORD will deliver him in time of trouble.

PSALM 41:1

Father, today I pray for those who are struggling with poverty, those in my own community and throughout the world. Let me not fall into the trap of considering the poor as different from myself, for You know how rapidly fortunes can change and the wealthiest can fall into difficulty. Help me be generous with both my donations and my efforts to help those in need. The little I can contribute seems ineffective, but You will multiply it because I am Your child and precious in Your sight.

PREJUDICE

Thou shalt not avenge, nor bear any grudge
against the children of thy people,
but thou shalt love thy neighbour as thyself:
I am the LORD.

LEVITICUS 19:18

Jesus, You have taught me that to live in heaven forever with You, I must be a good neighbor. Your parable about the Samaritan who offered aid shows that every person should be treated with kindness, even people that others might hate or despise because of their language, skin color, or place of birth.

Lord, so that I can live with You in heaven, give me the determination to act upon the truth that all people are equal in Your sight. Let me show kindness to everyone, because all are created in Your image.

PUTTING ON CHRIST'S IMAGE

You have put off the old man with his deeds,
and have put on the new man who is
renewed in knowledge according to
the image of Him who created him.

COLOSSIANS 3:9–10 NKJV

Lord, I'm being renewed, according to Your promise. As I grow in knowledge of You, I become more like You every day.

Some days I don't feel much like You, Lord, when I struggle to do Your will. But other days, I begin to see the changes You've made in my heart. I rejoice in that new me. But I ask You: Help me not to become proud about the reconstruction and give myself the credit. I know only You could make these heart alterations.

In all things make me into Your image, Lord. I need the change so much.

A READY HARVEST

Pray ye therefore the Lord of the harvest,
that he will send forth labourers
into his harvest.

MATTHEW 9:38

Father, even from my limited gardening experience, I've seen that weeds grow without encouragement, but good crops require attention. Seeds must be planted in soil that has been prepared to receive them, weeds must be eliminated, and produce must be harvested at the right time.

Almighty Savior, I see that the same sequence is necessary to produce a spiritual harvest. Lord, make me a faithful worker in Your harvest. Help me to be diligent in the work that brings the lost to You. May I have an urgency to gather souls into Your kingdom before the season is past and the crop is lost.

REAL DANGERS

Wherefore gird up the loins of your mind,
be sober, and hope to the end for the grace
that is to be brought unto you
at the revelation of Jesus Christ.

1 PETER 1:13

Sometimes danger is too real. A child becomes dangerously ill, a relative has a stroke, or someone we love is in an accident. We all react differently to such disasters, but eventually we all fall apart. Even those who seem strong as a rock shake on the inside. Somehow we manage to cope, to hold ourselves together and do what needs to be done in spite of our fear and grief. We live in hope: first in hope of a cure, then, if that fails, in hope of salvation. When all hope seems to be lost, Lord, be with those who suffer. Help them to never abandon hope, for all things are possible with You.

RESPONSIBILITY

While we look not at the things which are seen,
but at the things which are not seen:
for the things which are seen are temporal;
but the things which are not seen are eternal.

2 CORINTHIANS 4:18

Father, when I was young, some children would excuse their failures or belittle someone else's successes by saying, "In a hundred years no one will remember this." Now, that comment allows me to contrast trivial and important matters. Significant comments and actions have a way of reaching beyond the present and affecting eternity.

Lord, let me never take lightly my responsibility to dedicate my words and actions to You. Use what I say and do to influence someone to seek eternity with You in heaven. Today I trust that I have done all I could for You.

THE REWARD

Then shall thy light break forth as the morning,
and thine health shall spring forth speedily:
and thy righteousness shall go before thee;
the glory of the LORD shall be thy reward.

ISAIAH 58:8

You promise me wonderful rewards when I am charitable, Lord. I will be "like a watered garden, and like a spring of water, whose waters fail not" (Isaiah 58:11). Good health will come to me, as well as good reputation; and I will live a life of righteousness. Remind me of this the next time I pass up a charity event for an evening in front of the television set or hang up the telephone without even listening to the caller. I cannot answer every request made of me, so I count on You to guide me as to where I should invest my efforts in such a way as to bring You glory.

RIGHTEOUSNESS

The LORD openeth the eyes of the blind:
the LORD raiseth them that are bowed down:
the LORD loveth the righteous.

PSALM 146:8

Thank You, Lord God, for opening my eyes to see Your righteousness and raising me from my sin to new life in You. Without You, I would be blind and bowed down by sin. But Your love changed my life from the ground up.

On my own, I am never righteous. Certainly You could never love me for my deeds. Yet in Your generous, gracious love, You cared for me even when I ignored You.

Help me to love others as You have loved me. I want to be part of Your mission to open blind eyes and raise bowed-down hearts.

THE SALVATION OF ALL

For this is good and acceptable
in the sight of God our Saviour;
Who will have all men to be saved,
and to come unto
the knowledge of the truth.

1 TIMOTHY 2:3–4

Loving Father, only You know what is in a person's heart; only You are able to judge and save. You say it is Your desire that all should be saved and know Your truth, that through Your Son You have made salvation available to me if I but ask for it. I thank You for this greatest blessing of all.

Remind me that I am not Your gatekeeper or Your judge. My task is to spread the joyful gospel to all, to believe You will make my efforts fruitful, and never to stand in the way of another's salvation. Open my heart, show me where I am needed, and I will trust the rest to You.

A SEAT AT THE TABLE

Use hospitality one to another without grudging.

1 PETER 4:9

Hospitality involves an effort, whether it's a dinner party for twelve or throwing another potato in the stew for a child who doesn't want to eat at home that night. Hospitality means greeting newcomers after church services, maybe giving them the name of a good baby-sitter or pizza place. It means going to my child's piano recital and applauding every child, not just my own. It is doing little kindnesses cheerfully.

Lord, You welcomed me into Your family with love and acceptance. I was not worthy of Your hospitality, but You found me a seat at the table and fed me with Your Word. Help me be as kind to others as You have been to me—cheerfully welcoming everyone who wishes to dine with me tonight.

SELF-DISCIPLINE

For God did not give us a spirit of timidity,
but a spirit of power,
of love and of self-discipline.

2 TIMOTHY 1:7 NIV

As You grow my faith, Lord, You've made me aware that serving You shouldn't be a hit-or-miss thing—an option among others—but my life goal. Every choice I make should boldly work to forward Your kingdom, not my own self-interest.

I don't have to take that bold stance alone. Even when I lack strength to do the right thing, to make a choice that will be good for many days instead of just one, You help me decide well. When I'd like to go for the short-term benefit, Your Spirit reminds me I'm not only living for today—there's eternity to consider.

In You I have a spirit of power, love, and the self-discipline that obedience requires. Help me to live faithfully only for You, Lord.

SELF-HELP

"But the word of the LORD endures forever."
Now this is the word
which by the gospel was preached to you.

1 PETER 1:25 NKJV

Father, around the office I see people carrying self-help books to read during their lunch breaks. Each month another title makes the best-seller list. Yet, few have enough substance to be enduring classics.

Lord, when I study my human nature, I find many constants in my character—I am sinful, selfish, full of pride, sometimes afraid, and always facing death. The Bible addresses all these issues. Your Word is more thorough than any contemporary book that would try to show me how to improve myself without Your assistance. May I always remember to turn to Your enduring guidebook for daily living and eternal salvation.

SHARING

And God will generously provide all you need.
Then you will always have everything you need
and plenty left over to share with others.

2 CORINTHIANS 9:8 NLT

Lord, You've given me so much. Thank You for the generous way You've cared for all my needs. Though I may not always have a lot of extra money in the bank, my true necessities are always covered. And I'm continually rich in Your blessings.

Whatever I do have, Lord, help me share abundantly with others. I know that when I give out of what You've blessed me with, You always replenish my store. Whether my need is cash, food, or a place to live, I can trust in Your faithfulness every day.

Thank You for being ever faithful, Father. Your generosity blesses my life.

SIN FORGIVEN

*"Blessed is the man whose sin
the Lord will never count against him."*

ROMANS 4:8 NIV

Before I knew You, Lord, I could not understand the blessings of forgiven sin. But Your Spirit's cleansing and the freedom that followed faith are more wonderful than I could ever have imagined. Nothing the world offers can take their place.

Thank You for not counting my sin against me, but instead sending Your Son to take my place on the cross. If You'd left me to pay the price for my own wrongs, new life would have been impossible. But because You've put my sin away from me, everything's changed. Your pardon affects every corner of my being.

I'm totally blessed by Your forgiveness, Lord. Thank You from the bottom of my soul.

A SONG OF PRAISE

The LORD is my strength and my shield;
my heart trusted in him, and I am helped:
therefore my heart greatly rejoiceth;
and with my song will I praise him.

PSALM 28:7

I sing to You, O Lord, a continual song of praise. I declare Your name to all those who come into my presence. Words of thanksgiving are forever upon my lips. I can sing a new song because of Your grace and power. Your holy name is exalted in heaven and on earth, O Lord Most High. Your righteousness causes my heart to rejoice and break forth in a song of praise: "Glory to the God of my salvation. The generosity of Your compassion overwhelms my soul."

STEADFAST FAITH

"Therefore I say to you,
whatever things you ask when you pray,
believe that you receive them,
and you will have them."

MARK 11:24 NKJV

I'm so glad that all I have to do is believe, and I can receive the best from Your hand, Lord. But sometimes that believing is harder than it sounds. So many things—even good ones—can slide between my belief and the words I speak. Doubts often come to me more easily than faith.

On my own, I'm not very good at trusting You when life turns black. I tend to forget this verse or doubt that it's really for me. That's when I need to realize that my eyes are on the wrong thing—this world—when they should be on You.

Keep me steadfastly looking at You, Lord. Then I'll have all I could ask for.

SUFFERING

*"Do not fear any of those things
which you are about to suffer.
Indeed, the devil is about to throw
some of you into prison,
that you may be tested,
and you will have tribulation ten days.
Be faithful until death,
and I will give you the crown of life."*

REVELATION 2:10 NKJV

Not fearing suffering seems impossible, Lord. Suffering is not something any Christian looks forward to, yet all of us experience it in some way. Still, I know You have brought faithful believers through much more than I've experienced.

I haven't been imprisoned for my faith, Lord; but You promise You'll be there even if that should happen. Then if I stay faithful for a short time, I'll receive Your eternal crown of life and rejoice with You in heaven.

No matter what I suffer, keep me faithful to You, Jesus. I don't want anything to harm our relationship.

TEACHING ABOUT JESUS

These are the things that ye shall do;
Speak ye every man the truth
to his neighbour;
execute the judgment of truth
and peace in your gates.

ZECHARIAH 8:16

Lord Jesus, I occasionally take on the role of teacher, although I often feel inadequate for the task. My goal is to be a mentor, guide, and advisor. May I grow in knowledge, wisdom, character, and confidence so I can help those I teach to choose the proper path.

Heavenly Teacher, provide me with the ability to instill in my students a love for learning more about You, reading the Bible, talking to You in prayer, and living a life in keeping with Your Word. May I have an influence that will last a lifetime.

TONGUE FOLLOWS HEART

Before a word is on my tongue
you know it completely, O LORD.

PSALM 139:4 NIV

I can't keep a secret from You, Lord, because every word I speak is part of an open book. Before a syllable falls off my tongue, You know my thoughts and emotions. Words can't consistently hide feelings; eventually they'll directly reflect my heart and soul. In a sentence that shows what I really feel, truth finally comes out.

When I follow You closely, I need not worry. My words glorify You. Yet when I stray from You, my language changes, and people observe the alteration in my heart. Only if my heart is Yours will my words be, too, Lord. May both constantly focus on You.

UNEARNED GRACE

And I will have mercy upon her
that had not obtained mercy;
and I will say to them
which were not my people,
Thou art my people;
and they shall say, Thou art my God.

HOSEA 2:23

O Lord, how great is Your mercy to me. You owed me nothing because I paid You no heed, yet You called me. When I walked far from You, You called me to turn to Your path.

Thank You for caring for me when I wallowed in sin. I did nothing to earn Your grace, yet You gave it to me anyway. May Your great mercy be reflected in my life as I pass on mercy to those who sin against me. May mercy flow freely in my life.

UNFAILING LOVE

Love never fails.

1 CORINTHIANS 13:8 NKJV

I couldn't call my love for others "unfailing," Lord. When people irritate me, it's so easy to make unloving choices. Though I want to draw others to You by my own faithfulness, my own sin gets in the way; and I find myself being a traitor to Your kingdom.

Though my caring ability fails often, I know from experience and Your Word that Yours never does. I'm incredibly glad of this promise because I know how much I need Your love every moment of my life. If You failed to shower me with Your affection, my days would really be a mess.

Fill me with Your unfailing love for both those I relate to easily and those who are a challenge just to be with. Love them through me with Your unending compassion.

UNWORTHINESS

If we confess our sins,
he is faithful and just to forgive us our sins,
and to cleanse us from all unrighteousness.

1 JOHN 1:9

On my worst days I feel totally unworthy. I gather up my little pile of sins like dirty laundry and shake them toward the sky. "How can You possibly forgive this sin?" I ask, repeating the process until all my sins have been displayed. On my best days I calmly confess my sins (the exact same sins I had the day before), accept Your forgiveness, and go on with my life without guilt. I suspect that both reactions to guilt are acceptable, however. Confession is confession no matter how I phrase it. You have promised to cleanse me from all unrighteousness, to wipe away my guilt and make me whole if I confess my sins, and I thank You on both my good and bad days.

VALUED BY GOD

"And the very hairs on your head
are all numbered.
So don't be afraid;
you are more valuable to him than
a whole flock of sparrows."

LUKE 12:7 NLT

Sparrows aren't very important, Lord, yet You take care of even these small birds. Though some people may think them a nuisance, You know when each one falls.

Maybe it's not a huge compliment to be compared to sparrows, but I get Your message loud and clear. Everything about me, even down to how many hairs are on my head, is important to You. If You care about the birds, how much more important am I to You.

Thank You for having compassion even about the tiny things in my life. With that kind of concern, You're teaching me that I don't have to worry about a thing.

VICTORY

Therefore, my beloved brethren,
be ye stedfast, unmoveable,
always abounding in the work of the Lord,
forasmuch as ye know that your labour
is not in vain in the Lord.

1 CORINTHIANS 15:58

In my daily work, I rarely experience victory. I clean up one mess and move on to the next, knowing even greater messes are just around the corner. I never really seem to get anywhere, to win any battles, or see anything truly completed. There are precious few victories in my work. But You encourage me to hang in there and keep on working for You, because You have already won the victory in the most important battle of all—the battle for my soul. My daily problems come and go, yet if I remain steadfast and dedicated, doing the work You have given me to do, I am confident that my reward awaits me. Thank You, Lord.

WALKING IN WISDOM

And he will teach us of his ways,
and we will walk in his paths.

ISAIAH 2:3

You have promised me that I can know Your ways and walk in them, Lord. What a blessing that is to me, for I cannot know You more closely unless I know how You want me to live and can follow in Your footsteps.

I may not always be sure of my path. But I can be sure of You; as I continue to seek Your way, You will lead me to the right goal.

You, Lord Jesus, are always my goal. You are the end of my path; my eternal reward is to live with You forever. Thank You that my way leads to Your eternal home.

WALKING WITH GOD

Noah was a just man
and perfect in his generations,
and Noah walked with God.

GENESIS 6:9

Lord, I am defined by whom I choose as my heroes and whom I pattern my life after. Others interpret my character by those with whom I walk. I want to be like the heroes of old, those people of renown in the Old Testament who were described as having "walked with God."

Dear Father, give me the determination to walk at Your side. I seek an honorable walk that shows Your power and character. I know that I am not walking alone; You are with me. I have victory over impossible circumstances because I have placed myself in Your footsteps.

WASTING TIME

Favour is deceitful, and beauty is vain:
but a woman that feareth the LORD,
she shall be praised.

PROVERBS 31:30

I know friends come and go, whether they are rich
and powerful or just ordinary people. Currying
favor with the "right people" is rarely worth the trouble. They have nothing I want and will soon move on
to other friends because I have nothing they want.
Seeking personal beauty is likewise a waste of time. I
may be able to hide the toll of time for a little while,
but eventually the wrinkles will prevail. Help me
invest my precious time in more worthy pursuits,
Lord, ones that will provide lasting satisfaction. I'm
not sure what You will ask of me, but I am willing to
try anything You recommend and give any resulting
praise to You, where it belongs.

WISDOM
AGAINST STRIFE

Mockers stir up a city,
but wise men turn away anger.

PROVERBS 29:8 NIV

Plenty of people can tear down, but building up a leader so that problems can be solved is a better solution, Lord. I recognize that. Yet I've found it easy enough to criticize or condemn a boss, a politician, or a church leader.

Instead of rushing to attack a person or a situation, I want to become a problem solver—one who turns to You for the right, peaceful solution. So move my heart far from anger and hurt, and give me Your peace to share with others. Help me not to mock them, but to turn aside anger and find a real solution. Then I know I'll be doing Your will.

WITHOUT WAVERING

Let us hold fast the profession of
our faith without wavering;
(for he is faithful that promised).

HEBREWS 10:23

Lord, with Your blood You wiped away my sins, leaving me promises to enjoy in faith until You come back again to claim me as Your own. It takes patience to live in faith, and I confess that sometimes my patience runs thin. I wonder why You don't act in ways that I can see and understand. Why is there so much evil and suffering in this world that discourage both the faithful and the unfaithful? I don't understand. Help me realize that my understanding is not necessary for the completion of Your plan. You understand everything; all I need to do is have faith. In the meantime, keep me free from wavering, Lord. Your faithfulness is perfect, and Your will will be done.

THE WORK
OF OUR HANDS

And let the beauty of
the LORD our God be upon us:
and establish thou the work
of our hands upon us;
yea, the work of our hands establish thou it.

PSALM 90:17

What I do for a living can be either secular or sacred. The choice is mine. The kind of work I do is not important. I can do anything in a way that glorifies You, Father. A worker in the humblest of jobs is just as capable of demonstrating Your beauty as one in the most exalted of positions. The next time I am feeling unproductive or unappreciated, remind me that I am working for Your glory, not my own. A tiny bit of Your beauty is reflected in my work, whatever it might be. May those I work with always see You in my life and be brought closer to You through me.

WORLDLY POSSESSIONS

But thou shalt remember the Lord thy God:
for it is he that giveth thee
power to get wealth,
that he may establish his covenant
which he sware unto thy fathers,
as it is this day.

DEUTERONOMY 8:18

I don't think of what I have as wealth, Lord; it isn't enough to buy out a major corporation. But You've given me enough to fulfill Your covenant. You've cared for me every day of my life. I haven't appreciated enough how You've taken care of me or the way You have kept me going, even in rough times.

You've also given me countless spiritual blessings: a church to worship in, Christian friends, and Your love.

Thank You for the spiritual and financial wealth You've given me. I want to use it to Your glory. Show me how to spend it for You this day.

WORRY

Therefore take no thought, saying,
What shall we eat? or, What shall we drink? or,
Wherewithal shall we be clothed?
. . . for your heavenly Father knoweth that
ye have need of all these things.

MATTHEW 6:31–32

Worry is our most useless emotion. It is unproductive and dangerous. Sometimes it may
prod me into taking action to save myself, but even
then there is no guarantee that my actions will be
effective because I do not think rationally when I am
consumed with worry. Most of the time, worry dis-
ables me, locks me in my room, separates me from
those who would be willing to help. It convinces me
that I am unworthy, or stupid, or unforgiven—all lies
of the devil, not Your judgments. Being concerned
about my future is one thing; letting worry cripple
me is a lack of faith. You know what I need, Lord,
and You will provide.

WRONG IDEAS

As the Scriptures say,
"I will destroy human wisdom and
discard their most brilliant ideas."

1 CORINTHIANS 1:19 NLT

You know how much we treasure our ideas, Lord. The things we think—the beliefs we hold—are precious to us. But You promise us that human ideas are limited, and even our most brilliant ones pale compared to Your power.

When other people's bright ideas would hurt me, I'm glad You're still in control. It's comforting to know that nothing gets past You or is beyond Your control. But help me to remember that Your power also limits my human wisdom. When I think I'm being the smartest, my idea could be valueless if it doesn't side with Your wisdom.

Keep me in Your wise ways, Lord. I don't want my best ideas discarded because they were dead wrong.

If you enjoyed

PRAYERS & promises

be sure to check out the following books,
also available from Barbour Publishing, Inc.

Daily Prayers & Promises
Devotional Journal
ISBN 1-59310-025-6
Hardback, 384 pages, $19.97

Prayers & Promises
for the Graduate
ISBN 1-58660-831-2
Padded Hardback, 224 pages, $7.97

Prayers & Promises
for Men
ISBN 1-58660-833-9
Printed Leatherette, 224 pages, $4.97

Prayers & Promises
for Women
ISBN 1-58660-832-0
Printed Leatherette, 224 pages, $4.97

AVAILABLE WHEREVER BOOKS ARE SOLD